PREPARING
For The **King**

Christopher Bomford

ABOUT THE PUBLISHER

McKnight & Bishop are always on the lookout for new authors and ideas for new books. If you write or if you have an idea for a book, please email:
info@mcknightbishop.com

Some things we love are undiscovered authors, open-source software, Creative Commons, crowd-funding, Amazon/Kindle, faith, social networking, laughter and new ideas.
Visit us at **www.mcknightbishop.com**

Copyright © Chris Bomford 2023

The rights of Chris Bomford to be identified as the Author of this Work has been asserted by him in accordance with Section 77 of the Copyright, Designs and Patents Act 1988.

All rights reserved. No part of this book may be reproduced, stored on a retrieval system or transmitted in any form or by any means without prior permission in writing of the publisher nor be otherwise circulated in any form of binding or cover other than that in which it is here published without a similar condition being imposed upon the subsequent purchaser.

The views expressed in this work are solely those of the author and do not necessarily reflect the views of the publisher, and the publisher hereby disclaims any responsibility for them.

All Scripture quotations, unless otherwise indicated, are taken from the Holy Bible, New International Version®, NIV®. Copyright ©1973, 1978, 1984, 2011 by Biblica, Inc.™ Used by permission of Zondervan. All rights reserved worldwide. www.zondervan.com The "NIV" and "New International Version" are trademarks registered in the United States Patent and Trademark Office by Biblica, Inc.™

ISBN 978-1-905691-77.7

A CIP catalogue record for this book is available from the British Library.

First published in 2023 by McKnight & Bishop Inspire, an imprint of:

>McKnight & Bishop Ltd
>35 Limetree Avenue, Kiveton Park, South Yorkshire, S26 5NY
>http://www.mcknightbishop.com | info@mcknightbishop.com

This book has been typeset in Garamond, Gotham Thin, Ink Free

Printed and bound in Great Britain by
Mixam UK Ltd. 6 Hercules Way, Watford, Hertfordshire WD25 7GS

CONTENTS

Introduction 5

Chapter 1: The Bible Story: From Creation To The Cross   9

Chapter 2: The Bible Story: The Cross Until The End Of Time   19

Chapter 3: God's Plan Of Restoration   29

Chapter 4: How Should We Be?   43

Chapter 5: What Should We Do?   51

Chapter 6: What Is Our Message?   59

Chapter 7: Final Thoughts   63

About The Author   65

INTRODUCTION

We live in an age of increasing anxiety about where the world is heading. Our media feeds us an endless commentary on global issues that have the potential to negatively impact our lives and even threaten the very existence of life itself. The list of serious concerns seems endless. I can remember when the only environmental worry seemed to be the damage to the ozone layer! We were told this was serious but with the right response the situation could be recovered. It seems that this reassurance was valid as actions taken have begun the healing of the atmosphere with the prospect of a complete recovery by the second half of the century. However the current list of concerns have taken on apocalyptic dimensions: Global warming, disease pandemics, catastrophic wars, economic meltdown, environmental disaster and more. All of these are real and do represent a threat to life as we know it. In our selfish pursuit of health, wealth and prosperity we have left a legacy of enormous problems to the next generation. But is this the whole story and is there hope for a different ending? Is there a bigger picture God wants us to see?

The world is consumed with efforts to rescue the deteriorating situation. There are global summits, international agreements and commitments in response to scary scientific data and increasingly militant protests. But the world seems unable (and in some cases unwilling) to turn the tide of all this. To put it bluntly, man will not be able to fix it because it has consistently failed to be responsible stewards of God's creation. Furthermore, it doesn't want to accept or even hear what God has said about the future of the world. The Bible is very clear, the world won't

INTRODUCTION

go on for ever. There is an end to life as we know it today. There will be no utopia of peaceful and prosperous times. This is a stark truth that challenges our natural desire for things to get back to 'normal' (an often heard comment during the Covid pandemic). It also needs to be said that for some normal life was always wretched and all the doom saying has done is to extinguish any hope of a better future.

It is time to inject some hope here! God has a plan (not man) to redeem, restore and recreate the world. Although there will be major cosmic events and upheaval the end result will be more glorious than we can ever imagine. Everything that takes place will revolve around the person of God's Son, the Lord Jesus Christ. In short, the King is coming to planet earth not as a baby this time but as the glorious King of Kings and He will be seen by all the world. The Son of God is coming to claim His inheritance.

While the world has a sense of urgency about averting disaster, the church must avoid being sucked into this spiral of despairing action as though God has no plan for the future of mankind. Do we know what the Bible actually says about what will unfold in the end times? Do we have a confident expectation of the return of the Lord Jesus to bring the world under His authority and rule? Or have we become like those who say *"Where is this 'coming' he promised? Ever since our fathers died, everything goes on as it has since the beginning of creation." (2 Peter 3 v 4)*. Are we awake to the hour we live in and are we reading the signs of the times correctly?

There is no avoiding the fact that the Bible says there will be difficult days ahead in the world as evil will seem to be unrestrained. However, God's people are encouraged to not despair but hold fast to the promises of salvation. When we believe in Jesus as our Lord and Saviour we have been saved, we are being saved and we will be saved! Evil will not triumph, justice and righteousness are coming.

This book is not a comprehensive study of end time doctrine. There is a wealth of other resources that can help us interpret what is coming. My aim is to explore what the Bible says about how we can prepare for the coming of King Jesus. How should we be (our attitude)? What should we do (our actions)? And what is our message to the world? It must be about more than understanding the times as we need to know how to apply it. I see this in the difference between pure and applied mathematics. Pure maths is the theory while applied maths is how you can use it. We need to not only understand end time doctrine but what to do with it. To be like the men of Issachar *'who understood the times and knew what Israel should do' (1 Chronicles 12 v 32)*. The purpose of this book is to provoke us to understand what we should do in the light of our present times.

To get everything in context it will be necessary to outline the Bible story from creation to the end of time to give us the big picture of what God has been doing over the ages and will yet do. This will help us interpret the signs of what is to come. There are of course different interpretations of end time events and I'm not going to discuss the pros and cons of every doctrinal position. For the purpose of this book I will work with what I consider to be the original church view and one most consistent with Scripture. I will sketch this out in a later chapter. This book is based on three specific events to come that are promised in the Bible:

1. Jesus will come for His church (the rapture)

2. Jesus will return to rescue His people Israel from annihilation

3. Jesus will establish a 1000 year reign on earth together with us

One thing is sure, we are living in times of unprecedented turmoil. But this is also a period of time that the Bible has a lot to say about and it is for our benefit. Even creation itself is anticipating the fulfilment of the ages: *'The creation waits in eager expectation for the sons of God to be revealed.' (Romans 8 v 19).* Also the faithful, who have gone before, are waiting to receive their full inheritance: *'These were all commended for their faith, yet none of them received what had been promised. God had planned something better for us so that only together with us would they be made perfect' (Hebrews 11 v 39-40).* This is not just about us who are alive today, it is much bigger than that. It is about *'Your kingdom come, your will be done on earth as it is in heaven' (The Lord's prayer).* World events today are the fulfilment of long standing Bible prophecies. They indicate that the time of the return of King Jesus is near. When He talked to the disciples about what would happen before the end of the age, He told them to read the signs of the times and keep watch. He also said *'So you also must be ready, because the Son of Man will come at an hour when you do not expect him' (Matthew 24 v 44).* We don't know the exact time of His return but He wants us to be ready. I am convinced it is time to be expectant of His return.

The message of this book is that King Jesus is coming and we need to prepare for Him. My hope is that it can stir us up to be ready for His return.

Christopher Bomford
January 2023

CHAPTER 1:
THE BIBLE STORY:
FROM CREATION
TO THE CROSS

Before we look at what the Bible says about the coming of King Jesus, it will be helpful to step back for a moment to see the big picture. I want to put into context the events that are coming up which will radically change human history and bring to fulfilment God's purposes for His creation. In this chapter we will look at what has been the key purpose in His dealings with man in the period from creation to the cross. Together with the many different stories and lessons, there is a particular thread that runs through the Old Testament which is crucial for our salvation. As always, it concerns the birth into the world of the Lord Jesus who came to make a way back to God and give us an eternal future with Him. This has all been laid out for us in the Bible.

The Bible is extraordinary and unique in its composition. Just think about it for a moment, there are 66 books (39 in Old Testament and 27 in New) written by many different writers but with one source of inspiration: *'All Scripture is God-breathed and is useful for teaching, rebuking, correcting and training in righteousness, so that the man of God may be thoroughly equipped for every good work.' (2 Timothy 3 v 16-17)*. It is God the Holy Spirit who is the true author of Scripture, men were scribes who committed it into writing for us. This makes the Bible the only reliable source of truth for us. It is also the most comprehensive and complete record of

CHAPTER 1: THE BIBLE STORY: FROM CREATION TO THE CROSS

God's dealings with mankind covering the past, present (yes, the Bible is up to date) and future. From Genesis (the book of beginnings) to Revelation (the book of fulfilment) it is the story of restoration and redemption. It shows the faithfulness of God to keep His promises and above all it is about the Redeemer. It is the beautiful story of God's love, mercy and grace revealed to us in the sending of His Son, the Lord Jesus Christ.

An illustration of the wealth of prophetic insight in the Old Testament is revealed after Jesus had been raised from the dead and He caught up with two disciples on the road to Emmaus. They were downcast because they hadn't understood about what had happened to Him, so He opened their spiritual eyes for them: *'He said to them, "How foolish you are, and slow of heart to believe all that the prophets have spoken! Did not the Christ have to suffer these things and then enter his glory?" And beginning with Moses and all the Prophets, he explained to them what was said in all the Scriptures concerning himself.' (Luke 24 v 25-27)*. We have not only the Old Testament Scriptures that they had, but the revelation of the New Testament to help us understand the times and season we live in. We don't have to be 'foolish' or 'slow of heart to believe' for we not only have the complete written word but also the Holy Spirit who will lead us into all truth.

It is important to remember that the rapture of the church and the second coming of King Jesus to rescue His people Israel are not unexpected events, they are foretold in the Old Testament through prophecy. There are also types and shadows pictured in the lives of Bible characters that point to these things. God foreknew and planned all this. He gave us the Bible for a reason, He wants us to know and understand so that we are not caught by surprise by what is coming up. He doesn't want His people to be only spectators in what is unfolding, He wants us involved in its outworking. See how the apostle Paul put it: *'His intent was that now, through the church, the manifold wisdom of God should be made known to the rulers and authorities in the heavenly realms, according to his eternal purpose which he accomplished in Christ Jesus our Lord.' (Ephesians 3 v*

10-11). What an amazing truth. When we declare the gospel and all that God has planned, we are not only speaking to people but to the spiritual powers that control the world! That is why our enemy Satan not only wants to shut us up but to keep us ignorant of what God is going to do. The church is God's chosen way to reveal His wisdom today and remains our mandate until King Jesus comes.

So let us begin at the beginning. Genesis chapter 1 records how God created the heavens and the earth. God spoke into being everything we see around us and *'it was very good' (Genesis 1 v 31)*. There was the progressive creation of light, sky, land, seas, vegetation, trees, stars, sun, moon and every living creature imaginable all at His word. Finally, to crown His creation He made man in His own image. Someone to share life with and take care of the world for Him. God puts the first man, Adam into the Garden of Eden, a paradise in the centre of the earth to look after it. Right at the outset we see that relationship and purpose are two God given qualities for a fulfilling life and this is a constantly recurring theme of the Bible story. So to complete human relationship for Adam, He makes a woman out of his side and she is called Eve. At this point they are both naked but felt no shame, which pictures their state of innocence. And they lack nothing in Eden, the only restriction God put on them was that they must not eat from the *'tree of the knowledge of good and evil' (Genesis 2 v 16)*, if they did He warned them they would surely die. Clearly this didn't mean instant physical death as after Adam ate from that tree he went on to have children and subsequently lived for 930 years. It does of course include an eventual physical death but what is more serious is that it ruptured the relationship with God, which is a spiritual death. The breaking of an intimate friendship with God. This command to not eat from a specific tree now afforded Satan as God's arch enemy, an opportunity to tempt Adam and Eve to disobey God. And that is exactly what happened when Adam and Eve ate the forbidden fruit. Every human being has lived with the consequences of their disobedience and this is the root cause of all mankind's problems throughout the ages. We have all inherited from Adam a sinful nature that predisposes us to rebel against anything that impinges on our selfish desires. But God was not surprised by this and would now unveil His plan to redeem what looked like our hopeless situation.

When Adam and Eve fell for the temptation to disobey God it says they now realised they were naked, which pictures their loss of innocence. Now instead of enjoying the freedom of being in God's presence they hid themselves away from Him, which we can see as a snapshot of man's fallen condition (fearful of His judgement and ashamed of what they have done). God announces to Adam and Eve the consequences of their actions and confronts the serpent (Satan's agent) with a prophetic judgement: *"And I will put enmity between you and the woman, and between your offspring and hers; he will crush your head, and you will strike his heel." (Genesis 3 v 15)*. This powerful prophecy is the pivotal moment when God reveals His redemption plan. There is going to be a human being who will destroy Satan and all his works.

It is important to note that the agent of his destruction is human, which is confirmed by describing him as the 'offspring' or seed of the woman. This truth becomes relevant when we see what will now unfold. We know that this refers to God's own Son who is born of a woman into this world just like us so that He can legitimately represent mankind. The Son of God who becomes Son of Man for us. This the wonderful mystery of Jesus, perfectly man at the same time as completely God! The apostle John explains His mission like this: *'The reason the Son of God appeared was to destroy the devil's work.' (1 John 3 v 8)*. Satan caused this calamity and now God is going to reverse it. This announcement by God of Satan's fate has not only determined his end but put him on full alert as to the identity of who would 'crush his head'. His priority now is to find this person and destroy him before he can be destroyed. His attempts to do this shape what happens over the ages right up to the birth and beyond of our Saviour, the Lord Jesus Christ.

As a side note, there is something to see about what God did next with Adam and Eve. He made garments of skin to cover their nakedness, which would have required an animal sacrifice and the shedding of blood, a prophetic picture of the death of the Lord Jesus as the sacrifice for our sins. Then God ushered them away from the Garden of Eden and set an impenetrable guard in front of it saying, man *"must not be allowed to reach out his hand and take also from the tree of life and eat, and live for ever." (Genesis 3 v 22)*. This could look like punishment but it was in fact protection for us. If Adam in his fallen state, had eaten from the tree of life he would have lived forever in a sinful condition. That would have been disastrous for us as sin could never be put away, it would be permanent as there was no death to bring it to an end. In the book of Hebrews it explains: *'without the shedding of blood there is no forgiveness' (Hebrews 9 v 22)*. For sin to be dealt with a life had to be sacrificed and if there is no such thing as death it couldn't happen. Mankind would have been locked in a sinful state forever. A truly hopeless condition. God was again showing that His heart towards us is not to punish but to rescue us. He could have wiped the earth clean and started again but He didn't, He chose to redeem us. What love, what grace, what a wonderful God!

Back to the main point of this chapter. Satan is on the lookout for the one who will destroy him. Straight away we see evidence of this with Adam and Eve's first two sons, Cain and Abel. It says they both brought offerings to the LORD which evoked different responses. Abel sacrificed a firstborn animal from his flock as his offering (an echo of what God did to cover Adam's nakedness and prophetic picture of Jesus as the Lamb of God). But Cain brought produce from the soil (not a blood sacrifice and from the ground which God had cursed). Abel's offering pleased the LORD but Cain's did not, and as a result he was very angry at this rejection. Satan must have thought Abel was his nemesis, he was the son of Adam and Eve (*'offspring'* of the woman) and favoured by God. His opportunity to kill Abel came through Cain's anger and Satan was able to provoke him to murder his younger brother, which he did. This is jealousy pure and simple and reminds us how dangerous an emotion it is, it can lead to murder. We can see that jealousy is a motivation that Satan repeatedly uses in trying to stop God's plan to save us. Perhaps there is no surprise with this because that is precisely what led to Satan's downfall and rejection from heaven. The Bible reveals that in the beginning he was a dazzling angelic being (see Ezekiel 28 v 12-19) who wanted to make himself equal to God (see Isaiah 14 v 12-17). He was jealous of God and to this day is jealous of all who God favours. But Abel was not the one for Satan to find as God gave Eve another son called Seth in his place, and it is through his line that the Redeemer will come (see Luke 3 v 38).

As we move on we find that Satan switches tack in his attempts to frustrate God's redemption plan. Instead of targeting individuals he seeks to corrupt all of mankind so that it is beyond redemption. This is seen in the account of Noah's family and the flood when man's wickedness became so great that God was grieved that He had made man. There are differing views about what was happening here but I want to give you the interpretation which makes the best sense and fits the story of redemption. In Genesis chapter 6 it tells us that *'the sons of God'* married *'the daughters of men'* and had children by them. The children they produced were called *'the Nephilim'* and who are described as *'men of renown'*. In other words these individuals stood out from the crowd. These are mentioned again when Israel scouts the Promised Land and encounter inhabitants who are described as giants. Goliath at over nine feet tall would be a good illustration of this. What is happening here? The *'sons of God'* are fallen angels who were thrown out of heaven with Satan and the children they produced were part human, part angel. They were hybrids and not truly the *'offspring'* of the woman as announced by God. This was a serious attack on God's plan to redeem us. There is a possible reference to God's anger at this in the book of 2 Peter: *'God did not spare angels when they sinned, but sent them to hell, putting them in gloomy dungeons to be held for judgment; if he did not spare the ancient world when he brought the flood on its ungodly people, but protected Noah, a preacher of righteousness, and seven others ...' (2 Peter 2 v 4-5)*. If God was to preserve the purely human genetic line and ensure that redemption could be delivered He had to act and He chose Noah to save the situation. We have seen him described as *'a preacher of righteousness'* and in Genesis 6 it says *'he found favour in the eyes of the LORD' (v 8)* and is also *'a righteous man, blameless among the people of his time, and he walked with God' (v 9)*. We could say he was the last remaining good guy in a corrupt generation and that would seem to be what qualified him to be rescued along with his family. But there is something else important to see here. The word *'blameless'* used to described him can also, and is more usually translated as 'without defect'. In other words, Noah was one hundred percent human with no genetic corruption. By rescuing Noah and his family, God ensured that the line of redemption was secured. A perfect man would come to save us and destroy the works of the devil. There is an important lesson for us here, if Satan can't destroy he will try to corrupt. He won't be able to destroy the church but he will do all he can to corrupt it, and that is what has happened through the ages and is still happening today.

As we continue through the Bible record we can find many instances where Satan tried to derail God's plan to save us. It becomes clearer where the Redeemer will come from when God begins to choose individuals, families, tribes and the nation of Israel and make binding covenants with them. This revelation won't be lost on Satan. Let me highlight a few instances where God's plan of redemption was under attack.

The first significant covenant God makes is with an individual called Abram whose name means 'exalted father' but is later renamed Abraham which means 'father of many nations'. He had no children, his wife Sarai (later Sarah) was barren and they were both well past the age of parenthood. Nevertheless they had a promise from God that they would have an heir and the Redeemer would come from this family line. Abraham survived famine and the danger of being killed so men could get hold of his beautiful wife. The promised son Isaac is born and marries Rebekah to have two sons, Esau and Jacob. The youngest brother Jacob, through trickery gets the first born blessing and now steps into the family line of the redeemer. This enrages his older brother Esau who threatens to kill him, but his mother sends him away to safety. In time he has twelve sons but his favourite is Joseph who becomes a target of Satan. His brothers are jealous of him, they think of killing him but sell him into slavery. He survives prison and ends up saving his family from starvation. There are many pictures here of Jesus and the treatment by His own people Israel including their rescue when He will return and reveal Himself to them!

We can also think of how Egypt's Pharaoh was incited to kill all the baby boys born to Hebrew women which would have ultimately destroyed the nation of Israel and the Saviour's family line. But God pulled Moses from the reeds to lead the people of Israel out of slavery and into the Promised Land keeping them intact as a nation. Satan had failed again. We can also think of King Saul's hostility towards David. He became so jealous that he tried to kill him. That sounds familiar. By now it was becoming clearer from which family line the Redeemer would come and it made David a key target, emphasised when 'Son of David' was later understood in Israel to refer to the Saviour. Throughout Israel's history we can see continual hostility towards the nation with repeated attempts to wipe them out. The real culprit is Satan in his efforts to kill the One who would *'crush his head'*. He failed as God intervened whenever necessary to protect His plan of salvation. Nevertheless, Satan would have been aware of the increasing number of prophecies that gave more insight into God's plans and he wasn't going to give up on finding him.

This brings us to the moment of the Redeemer's arrival. Around one thousand years after King David, the Saviour is born in Bethlehem as prophesied, not in a palace but to an unknown young couple from Galilee. However, this obscurity wasn't to last as an angelic fanfare propelled shepherds to visit Jesus and afterwards they spread the word about all they had seen and heard. The news was getting out and it was going to reach the ears of King Herod when Magi from the east arrived enquiring about the arrival of the King of the Jews. Jealous of his position as king he orders the killing of all boys up to two years old in Bethlehem and the surrounding area. Again an echo, this time of Pharaoh's attempts to kill all Hebrew boys. But Joseph and Mary are warned in a dream and escape to Egypt only returning after Herod dies. A further dream leads them to safety in Galilee, out of reach of Herod's son. Let us pause for a moment to wonder at what God has done. The Saviour, God's own Son was born into a family like everybody else and not just dropped into the world as a fully grown man. Also, He was born into the humblest of surroundings with no armed guards or privilege. All of this would make Him vulnerable to the enemy's efforts to destroy Him and our hope of redemption. Truly He became just like us which means He can legitimately represent us as Son of Man.

The Redeemer is now on earth and grows up in Nazareth. The Bible says little about His early years apart from the time He went to Jerusalem for the Passover Feast when He was twelve years old. It simply says He *'became strong ... was filled with wisdom, and the grace of God was upon him' (Luke 2 v 40)*. The next significant event comes when He is baptised by John the Baptist in the River Jordan and at this moment God the Father speaks from heaven identifying Jesus as God's own beloved Son. Now Satan is in no doubt who will destroy him but he will not be able to defeat Him as the Son of God so he attacks Jesus as the Son of Man, that is in His humanity. He tempts Jesus in the wilderness to misuse His power, test His Father's protection and worship Satan with the prize of owning the world. Unlike in the Garden of Eden, these temptations fail and Jesus is perfectly obedient to the Father's plan for Him. The Bible then says *'When the devil had finished all this tempting, he left him until an opportune time' (Luke 4 v 13)*. The opportune time was to be the cross.

As Jesus approached His crucifixion we see Him putting aside all His divine power and authority so that He could be man's true representative before the judgment of our sins by God. As Son of God He could have wiped out all His enemies with a word and returned to His Father's side if He wished. Satan would have been eliminated but we would still be captive to sin so Jesus '... *became obedient to death – even death on a cross!*' *(Philippians 2 v 8)*. To secure salvation for us Jesus had to die as our sacrifice for sin. When He was crucified Satan must have thought he had won and that his Nemesis had gone but he was wrong. And he was yet to realise that he had lost and his fate had been sealed. This was just the beginning of his downfall and the losing of his grip on planet earth as we shall see in the next chapter.

The point of this chapter is to reveal the redemption thread that runs through the Old Testament and the gospels. Above all, it is the story of God's Son as our Redeemer. It is also a testimony of God's faithfulness to deliver His promise to send a man to crush the serpent's head and we have seen how He intervened to protect His plan to rescue us. Now redemption has come the emphasis of God's plans will shift to a new focus which we will now explore.

CHAPTER 2: THE BIBLE STORY: THE CROSS UNTIL THE END OF TIME

In the previous chapter we saw how the crucifixion of Jesus must have seemed like a victory to Satan, as the One who had come to destroy him and all his works was gone. But even at His death there were signs that all was not finished. There were extraordinary happenings as recorded in Matthew's gospel: *'At that moment the curtain of the temple was torn in two from top to bottom. The earth shook and rocks split. The tombs broke open and the bodies of many holy people who had died were raised to life'* (Matthew 27 v 51-52). The way into God's presence had been opened up and death had been conquered! This was not only confusing and disturbing to Israel's religious leaders but would have raised questions in Satan's mind as to whether he had really won. Any doubts would have gone when on the third day Jesus reappeared after His resurrection. I can imagine a shudder went through the ranks of God's enemies when they saw this. Something unimaginable had happened, the Son of God had died in our place so we could be made right with Almighty God and be able to live with Him forever. Man could now be promoted to heaven, the very place Satan was ejected from. The apostle Paul wrote: *'And God raised us up with Christ and seated us with him in the heavenly realms in Christ Jesus, in order that in the coming ages he might show the incomparable riches of his grace, expressed in his kindness to us in Christ Jesus.'* (Ephesians 2 v 6-7). Now His work on earth was finished Jesus returned to His Father's side and a new era of God's plan for the world began.

CHAPTER 2: THE BIBLE STORY: THE CROSS UNTIL THE END OF TIME

Christ's victory on the cross was final and has set the end of things. We are now living in the times of the progressive fulfilment of God's promises as we move towards the end of time. Satan as *'the prince of this world'* who *'now stands condemned'* (John 16 v 11) can't change his destiny of destruction. However, what he will try to do is frustrate, obstruct and delay God's plan if he can. His only opportunity to do this is by persecuting and corrupting the church. Most of all he wants to silence the preaching of the gospel so that people remain ignorant of salvation and join him in his destruction. Failing that, he wants to corrupt Bible truth and the image of church so that it seen as irrelevant, impotent and hypocritical. In many parts of the world Christians are under severe persecution and often have to remain hidden, but that has not stopped the church growing as the recent history of the Chinese church shows. The gospel always gets out somehow. In the western world the persecution is not so obvious as it is more about corrupting the message and pushing the church into apostasy (a denial of Bible truth).These are times of increasing opposition to what the Bible says as events move towards the return of King Jesus. Paradoxically, even in this hostile atmosphere there is a growing spiritual hunger that only Jesus can satisfy. The harvest is still on and it is time for the church to be aware of the season we are in and to know what we should do.

We are living in what the Bible calls the 'last days'. This was announced at the birth of the church when Peter stood up at Pentecost and quoted from the prophet Joel: *'In the last days, God says, I will pour out my Spirit on all people ...'* (Acts 2 v 17). These 'last days' will continue until *'the coming of the great and glorious day of the Lord'* (Acts 2 v 20). Joel's prophecy points to the day when the Lord Jesus will appear again on earth. Until then the promise is that *'everyone who calls on the name of the Lord will be saved'* (Acts 2 v21). The Holy Spirit has been given to empower the church to preach the gospel to all creation so that this can happen. This is called the Great Commission. The end of each of the gospels contains different aspects of this commission, in Matthew it is the instruction to make disciples of all nations, in Mark it tells us what happens when we do this, Luke gives us the content of the gospel message (repentance and forgiveness of sins) and in John that Jesus is sending us as the Father sent Him. All these instructions to the church still stand in this season and will do so until the Lord Jesus comes to call us up to be with Him forever, this is known as the rapture. There will be successive different eras that follow but we start by understanding what the key purpose of God is in this season.

We are now living in the time between the cross and the rapture of the church. It has been described as the 'gathering of the bride' with Jesus as the bridegroom and the church as the bride. Jesus alludes to this in a parable: *'The kingdom of heaven is like a king who prepared a wedding banquet for his son' (Matthew 22 v 2)*. God the Father is the king and Jesus is His Son. Servants are sent out to bring the guests to the wedding but they are unwilling. We should remember the context here as He is referring to Jews who at that time rejected Jesus as their Messiah. As the parable goes on to explain their rejection opened up the invite to anyone, in other words the whole world! However, this is not the end of the story for the people of Israel as we shall see later. Intriguingly, if we see the servants as believers preaching the gospel they also end up as the bride! There is a delightful story in the Old Testament that also pictures this idea of a father looking for a bride for his son. Abraham wanted a suitable wife for his son Isaac and he sends an unnamed servant to find her. After a journey back to Abraham's home country the servant meets Rebekah, a beautiful girl who becomes Isaac's wife. There is a lot in this story but the typology is clear, Abraham is God the Father, Isaac is Jesus, the servant is the Holy Spirit and Rebekah is the church. It is good to remember that more than anything else we are in a love story. But this time has not yet ended as the bride is still being gathered. There is another theme in this age which warrants its own chapter and it is how God has been at work restoring things that have been lost since the birth of the church. But now we will look at the next major event in God's plans, the rapture.

As we look beyond the church age we will find subjects that have become contentious and open to different interpretations. As I said in the introduction to this book, I am working with what I consider to be the original church view of the end times. Let us look at the evidence for the rapture which is when Jesus calls believers up to heaven to be with Him forever. Although the word rapture is not used in the traditional English Bible translations it can be found in Latin versions and is derived from the word 'raptura'. The clearest reference to this event is found in the apostle Paul's earliest letters which were to the Thessalonian church: *'For the Lord himself will come down from heaven, with a loud command, with the voice of the archangel and with the trumpet call of God, and the dead in Christ will rise first. After that we who are still alive and are left will be caught up together with them in the clouds to meet the Lord in the air. And so we will be with the Lord for ever.' (1 Thessalonians 4 v 16-17)*. This is plainly meant to be taken literally as a specific future event and the words *'caught up'* means the rapture. This the moment that the church is removed from the earth to be in heaven. This will trigger a series of dramatic events on a scale never seen before. Believers will also receive their resurrection bodies at this time which is described for us in 1 Corinthians 15. We will have bodies that are eternal and wonderfully beyond anything we have known before.

The removal of the church will have serious consequences for the world. Jesus calls the church *'the salt of the earth'* and *'the light of the world' (Matthew 5 v 13-14)*. The presence of believers on earth preserves (like salt) and is the only source of true light in the dark times we live in. Let me explain what I mean by preserving. Think of how God wouldn't destroy Sodom and Gomorrah until Lot (the only righteous man) and his family were brought out but as soon as they left judgment fell. The presence of the church on earth stays God's hand of judgment on all the wicked things that man does on earth but the world doesn't understand that. Paul's second letter to the Thessalonians highlights this as he had to reassure them that the rapture hadn't happened yet (they had received false reports). He writes: *'For the secret power of lawlessness is already at work; but the one who now holds it back will continue to do so till he is taken out of the way. And then the lawless one will be revealed, whom the Lord Jesus will overthrow with the breath of his mouth and destroy by the splendour of his coming.' (2 Thessalonians 2 v 7-8).* The most logical interpretation is that it is Spirit filled church that prevents the appearance of the Antichrist and rapture of the church will remove the last restraint before the world is plunged into a time that is called the Tribulation or 'Time of Jacob's Trouble' when the people of Israel are threatened with annihilation. We won't cover every detail in this time but it will be important to understand the key issues in God's redemption plan. The world will enter a time of conflicts and deception as Satan wars against God's purposes.

We will stick with the traditional interpretation of end time events which defines the Tribulation as a seven year period of global upheaval. The book of Daniel, particularly chapters 9 and 12 speak of this period. The end time teaching of Jesus to His disciples recorded in Matthew 24, Mark 13 and Luke 21 gives graphic details of what is to come, particularly for Israel. As is often pointed out if we want to know how near these things are then we should look at what is happening in and to Israel. They are back in their own land after nearly 2000 years of being dispersed throughout the world and they have regained control of Jerusalem. These are fulfilments of significant Biblical prophecies for the end times. It is also worth pointing out that Revelation chapters 6 to 19 detail what will happen during this time of successive judgments, but the church will not be there! It is in heaven waiting to return with King Jesus at the end of the Tribulation. The church, represented by the twenty four elders, are mentioned as being in heaven in chapters 5 and 6 which is before the events of the seven years begin.

During this seven year period the Antichrist will establish himself as the supreme world leader. He is imagined to be charismatic and so gifted that the world sees him as having the answer to all its problems and he will be supported by another demonic being who performs miraculous signs that deceive the world into serving and worshipping the Antichrist (see Revelation 13). During the first three and a half years of this time the people of Israel are able to rebuild the temple in Jerusalem but then the Antichrist *'will oppose and will exalt himself over everything that is called God or is worshipped, so that he sets himself up in God's temple, proclaiming himself to be God'* *(2 Thessalonians 2 v 4)*. The Antichrist will demand that all worship is to him alone and for complete submission by everyone on earth. This is what Jesus referred to when He told His disciples *"'So when you see standing in the holy place 'the abomination that causes desolation', spoken of through the prophet Daniel ...'"* *(Matthew 24 v 15)*. It also triggers what Jesus describes as *'great distress, unequalled from the beginning of the world until now – and never to be equalled again'* *(Matthew 24 v 21)*. The people of Israel will become the target of Satan's wrath and it will look as if they will be completely destroyed. Ezekiel chapters 38 and 39 are relevant prophecies of the attempt to destroy the people of Israel. However, Jesus also promised that those days would be cut short for the sake of the elect (see Matthew 24 v 22) and the Bible indicates that a remnant of the Jewish people will escape destruction by fleeing to the land of Edom, which is present day Jordan. Then, at the end of this time of global distress Jesus appears as KING OF KINGS AND LORD OF LORDS to overthrow all His enemies in what is called the battle of Armageddon and Satan is bound and thrown into the Abyss for a thousand years (see Revelation 19 and 20). The Lord Jesus has delivered His people Israel and judges those who persecuted them during the Tribulation, this is what is referred in Matthew 25 v 31-46. This brings those frightening seven years to a close and establishes the thousand year reign of the Lord Jesus on earth, referred to as the Millennium. There are of course other details which are not covered here.

The promise of a thousand year period when King Jesus rules on earth is based on verses in Revelation: *'Blessed and holy are those who have part in the first resurrection. The second death has no power over them, but they will be priests of God and of Christ and will reign with him for a thousand years.'*

(Revelation 20 v 6). This verse also says that believers will reign with the Lord Jesus as they are the ones who experienced the first resurrection, which happened at the rapture. The suggestion of a millennial rule is another subject which the church has argued about throughout ages. There are different interpretations depending on whether we take it literally or think of it as simply figurative. The figurative or allegorical viewpoint dismisses the idea that Jesus will actually come back to rule on earth, and it is the prevailing view in the mainline churches. Sadly, it opens the door to scepticism about many Old Testament prophecies concerning Jesus as the Son of David ruling from Jerusalem. Tragically it also fostered anti-Semitism as it downplays the significance of Jerusalem and land of Israel in God's plans of complete restoration. This view is called amillennialism meaning there is no thousand year reign on earth. As stated before, I am working with what I consider to be the original church view and that there is a millennium with Jesus ruling on earth from Jerusalem. See what the disciples asked Jesus before He ascended to heaven: *'Lord, are you at this time going to restore the kingdom to Israel?' (Acts 1 v 6).* They were clearly thinking of a literal restoration and freedom from Roman rule. Jesus didn't correct their thinking about this idea but simply told them they were not to know the times set by the Father. Also see what they were told when they saw Jesus ascending to heaven: *"Men of Galilee ... why do you stand here looking into the sky? This same Jesus, who has been taken from you into heaven, will come back in the same way you have seen him go into heaven"*. *(Acts 1 v 11).* The Lord Jesus will return to the Mount of Olives to commence His millennial rule. This is all meant to be taken literally and why the literal interpretation is a valid one.

As resurrected believers will also be on earth during this time it will be good to see what the Bible says it will be like. Most importantly, the world will at last be ruled by the Righteous King so there will be perfect justice for all. There are prophecies that paint a picture of a world so different to today. There will be peace among the nations (Isaiah 2), people will live long lives (Isaiah 65), wild animals will no longer attack each other or people (Isaiah 11) and *'the earth will be full of the knowledge of the LORD as the waters cover the sea' (Isaiah 11 v 9)*. We also remember that Satan is not on the scene so the world will know what it is like to be free from his temptations and provocations. However, this is not God's eternal destination for His people and there will still be death and sin present because not everyone will be a born again believer.

What happens next may seem surprising: *'When the thousand years are over, Satan will be released from his prison and will go out to deceive the nations in the four corners of the earth - Gog and Magog - to gather them for battle. In number they are like the sand on the seashore' (Revelation 20 v 7)*. The thought that people would still be deceived and rebel against God after the blessings of the millennium may strike us as strange. Perhaps it simply reveals that man is inherently rebellious unless they receive a new spirit. God puts down this final rebellion with fire from heaven and Satan will be sent to eternal destruction. This is followed by the final judgment of man at the *'great white throne' (Revelation 20 v 11)*. At this point we need to remember that all those who have already been redeemed will not appear here. Jesus Christ took the judgment for our sins at the cross and the only judgment we face is for our reward (see 2 Corinthians 5 v 10). God would be unjust to punish us for sins that He had already judged in His Son on the cross. God with perfect justice judges all remaining people and all those whose names are not recorded in the *'book of life' (Revelation 20 v 12)* join *'death and Hades'* in the lake of fire which is called *'the second death' (v 14)*. All this may seem uncomfortable to us but we have to recognise that God is a perfect and just judge whose heart is that no-one should perish. He is the creator and we are the created. In other words He is God and we are not!

Now we reach the finishing line of God's redemption plan. His enemies have been dealt with, sin has been paid for and man can live freely in the presence of God forever. The destination God has planned for man is a whole new beginning. Here is what the apostle John saw in his vision: *'Then I saw a new heaven and a new earth, for the first heaven and the first earth had passed away, and there was no longer any sea' (Revelation 21 v 1).* It goes on to say that man and God will now live together and that the struggles of this life will be a thing of the past: *'He* (God) *will wipe every tear from their eyes. There will be no more death or mourning or crying or pain, for the old order of things has passed away' (Revelation 21 v 4).* Everything is made new and evil has no place there. The vision contains a description of a glorious New Jerusalem which is of great size and made of pure gold with the river of life flowing throughout. We can only speculate about the meaning of all the details that are given but one day we will be there to see all this for ourselves! An intriguing fact about the Holy City is that it *'does not need the sun or the moon to shine on it, for the glory of God gives it light, and the Lamb is its lamp.' (Revelation 21 v 23).* Furthermore, it goes on to say there will be no night. The sun and the moon were created to give man a framework of time to live in, so if they are no longer there then time as we know it no longer exists. I see this as literally the end of time and the beginning of eternity.

The book of Revelation closes by returning to the image of the redeemed (church and remnant of Israel) as the bride of Christ and a note of eagerness is injected with the promise that Jesus is coming soon (see Revelation 22 v 12). This brings the response: *'The Spirit and the bride say, "Come!" And let him who hears say, "Come!"...' (Revelation 22 v 17).* The final words are *'Come, Lord Jesus' (Revelation 22 v 20)* to express our desire for the Lord Jesus, our wonderful Saviour and Bridegroom. I believe we need an awakening in the church of the desire and expectancy for the return of the KING OF KINGS AND LORD OF LORDS. Before we explore what that might mean in practice we will look at what has been God's plan of restoration for the church through the ages.

CHAPTER 3: GOD'S PLAN OF RESTORATION

The church was birthed at Pentecost when the Holy Spirit fell on the believers waiting in Jerusalem as Jesus had instructed them. They were now empowered to make Jesus known through the preaching of the gospel and the Holy Spirit would confirm the truth of their message with signs and miracles (see Mark 16 v 20). This was not what the powers of darkness wanted to happen and in an attempt to silence the church the early believers were severely persecuted. Ironically, the agents of this persecution were the religious leaders who were the very ones who said they were waiting for the Messiah. As we shall see, this is a pattern that is repeated throughout history. But this persecution could never destroy the church as Jesus had told His disciples: '... *I will build my church, and the gates of Hades will not overcome it*' *(Matthew 16 v 18)*. The church would come under great pressure but it would not be overcome. In the light of this, Satan now switches to corrupting the church and its message to render it ineffective in bringing people to salvation. As already mentioned in the opening chapter this is his usual way of attempting to disrupt God's redemption plan. As we shall now see, he has had some success with this as the church sank to a very low ebb for a time. This meant God repeatedly acted to restore the church to its original place as light and life to the world. God has always been in the business of restoring what has been lost and is the very purpose for which He sent His Son into the world. This is reflected in a promise He made to Israel *'So I will restore to you the years that the swarming locust have eaten...' (Joel 2 v 25 NKJV)*. We will now take a brief look at what has happened in church history and what it says to us today. What has God been restoring and what is yet to be restored before the rapture?

But before we do that, there is one last point to make about the foundations of the church. The roots of the church are Jewish, the original believers were Jews, our Saviour is King of the Jews and from the family line of King David of Israel. Much of the church ignores this truth, particularly when they think God has totally rejected the people of Israel forever and replaced them with the Gentiles (non-Jews). But He has not rejected Israel, they have been put to one side until the full number of the Gentiles have come into the Kingdom of Heaven (see Romans 11 v 25-32). As Gentiles, we owe the early Jewish believers a great debt because it is through them that the gospel came. God's redemption plan is for the church and Israel to come together in one new body, but more on that later. When we read the book of Acts it is clear that the gospel wasn't taken to Gentiles until chapter 10 when Peter went to a Roman centurion called Cornelius. Initially Peter was reluctant to do this as it seems that the disciples had forgotten that Jesus had told them *'... go and make disciples of all nations...' (Matthew 28 v 19)*. They thought salvation was reserved for the Jews alone and God had to correct that mindset. This episode teaches us that our prejudices are obstructive to the purposes of God and that we have to put what the apostle Paul said into practice *'Do not conform any longer to the pattern of this world, but be transformed by the renewing of your mind. Then you will be able to test and approve what God's will is – his good, pleasing and perfect will.' (Romans 12 v 2)*. This is why throughout church history we see God having to break into individual's lives to bring about the revival of His purposes. He challenges our thinking to restore the truths of salvation. He will finish what He has started and bring it to a good and glorious conclusion!

Reading the letters of apostles Paul and John we can see that there were many teething problems in the early church to do with behaviour and doctrine. For example, it appears that the church in Corinth was a very lively place, rowdy even. Corinth was a major city in Greece, a commercial crossroads with every kind of pagan practice and behaviour. Paul's letters had to confront the Corinthian believers as many were still behaving in the ways of the world and needed to see that they were called and empowered to live godly lives. Despite this Paul comments: *'Therefore you do not lack any spiritual gift as you eagerly wait for our Lord Jesus Christ to be revealed'* (1 Corinthians 1 v 7). What a picture of God's grace, it was their simple faith in Christ that qualified them for every spiritual gift not their behaviour, this a definite challenge to legalistic religious attitudes! Other letters of Paul and John confront and give guidance on many matters including attitudes towards other believers. We are to not think too highly of ourselves and be loving just as Christ loves us. This is timeless wisdom and relevant to today as we are made of the same stuff as the early church. While questionable behaviour in the church could undermine their witness to the world it was arguments over doctrine that were the most serious. Again, Satan's desire is to so corrupt the gospel message that it becomes ineffective in bringing people to salvation. The Holy Spirit will only move in signs and wonders when we are preaching the truth as He will not confirm error. We need to remember that it is His power not our persuasiveness that saves people that is why our enemy tries to distort the truths of the gospel.

Both Paul and Peter had to deal with the errors of false teachers who came into the church creating doubts and divisions over the apostles teaching. And John had to write a letter (1 John) exposing dangerous ideas questioning the identity of Christ, a believer's freedom and whether we are naturally sinful. All these errors were the work of antichrist spirits to try and render the gospel null and void, see what John said: *'Dear children, this the last hour; and as you have heard that the antichrist is coming, even now many antichrists have come. This is how we know it is the last hour'* (1 John 2 v 18). He goes on to reveal that these were people who had infiltrated the church but didn't really belong to them so had to leave. This can still happen today. John's purpose was to restore the truth of Christ's identity and godly living.

But the biggest battle was over the role of law in a Christian's life, in particular the Law of Moses. The Jewish believers grew up in a culture defined by the Law, it was not only their rules for living but also their very identity. Even though Jesus had fulfilled all the requirements of the Law for them (see Matthew 5 v 17) they struggled to step free from its strict demands and embraced a faith in Christ plus obedience to the Law. This attitude had a powerful influence on the doctrine in the early church which was going to cause trouble when Gentile believers joined them. Paul wrote his strongest letter to the Galatian church who were stuck in this mindset. He is withering in his condemnation saying they had been bewitched and stepped out of grace and back under the curse of the Law. But most seriously, they had alienated themselves from Christ as he told them: *'Mark my words! I, Paul, tell you that if you let yourselves be circumcised, Christ will be of no value to you at all. Again I declare to every man who lets himself be circumcised that he is required to obey the whole law. You who are trying to be justified by law have been alienated from Christ; you have fallen away from grace.' (Galatians 5 v 2-4)*. Getting circumcised was symbolic of putting yourself under the need to keep the Law. The requirement for believers to keep the Law as well faith in Christ nearly split the church in two and it was only the Council at Jerusalem that rescued the situation (see Acts 15). This is still an issue in the church today, although it has morphed into how we stay saved. Some argue that yes, we are saved by grace but now there are requirements (guidelines, rules, traditions etc.) that we need to keep to stay justified before God. Wrong! That is the same old trap of self-justification and God won't accept it. We are saved by grace to live by grace. This is why the book of Hebrews, although written primarily to Jewish background believers, is such a useful source of teaching on the dangers of legalism. The doctrine of having to live right to be acceptable to God is a weapon that Satan has continually used throughout history to bring condemnation both inside and outside the church. Jesus Himself told us that He didn't come to condemn but to save, Amen.

The book of Acts covers the first thirty years of church history, so what about the following nearly nineteen hundred years? It has been a time of restoration to bring the church back to its place of light, life and love. Once the first apostles had left the scene and under increasing persecution, it didn't take long before things started to slip. Arguments over church leadership, neglect of the ordinances of baptism and communion and the inroads of heresies such as Gnosticism weakened its understanding of the truth. Another factor was the destruction of Jerusalem in AD70 when the Jewish people were driven from their homeland, which effectively removed Jewish influence in the early church. Sadly, it also birthed an anti-Semitic attitude in the now largely Gentile church. But moving on, in AD312 the Roman emperor Constantine converted to Christianity and made it the state religion. On the face of it this seemed good news, persecution began to diminish and it became fashionable to be a Christian (just like the emperor). But it was a masterstroke of Satan in his efforts to corrupt the church. Many pagan practices were Christianised to appear spiritually acceptable, including Christmas day which was previously celebrated as the birthday of the Sun! It also opened the door for other pagan ideas to enter church practices, such as ornate robes and headgear associated with other deities. The simplicity of the early church was being swept away by the state religion.

But God would faithfully act to restore the purity of the gospel by raising up many individuals throughout history to keep the lamp of truth burning. I think of John Wycliffe who translated the Latin Bible into English so everyone could read it for themselves. Until then people only had what the priest told them to go on, and that was controlling to say the least. Wycliffe had restored the understandable written word into the hands of everyone. The church hierarchy were furious at this because they had lost their power to control and manipulate their congregations, but it was too late as the word was out. There were of course many other people and groups who clung to the gospel truth and we are beneficiaries of their sacrifice because many of them paid with their freedom and even their lives. But there are two particular restorations that I want to mention as being key for the church.

The first is the Reformation. In the year 1517 a German Catholic priest was troubled by the sense of his sinfulness and the need to keep confessing his sins, until he read: *'For in the gospel a righteousness from God is revealed, a righteousness that is by faith from first to last, just as it is written: "The righteous will live by faith."'* *(Romans 1 v 17)*. The light came on for Luther and he saw he was justified before God by faith in Christ alone and not by his good works. But not only was he now free from condemnation he saw the corruptness of the Roman Catholic Church that pedalled a doctrine of works and yet more works. He was so incensed that he nailed 95 objections on the door of the church in Wittenburg which ignited a fire throughout Europe and birthed the Protestant reformation. Justification by faith alone had been restored to the doctrine of the church even though there was strong resistance and many counter attacks to come. The Reformation didn't restore all gospel truth at that time and anti-Semitism was still prevalent in the church. Nevertheless, God was step by step bringing the church back up to its proper place. Many revivals and movements followed around the world as God raised up men like John Wesley and George Whitfield to preach the gospel to a needy world.

The next significant event I am highlighting is the Pentecostal revival of the early 1900's. First there was the Welsh revival which began in 1904 and is reckoned to have resulted in over one hundred thousand people being saved and communities being transformed. News of all this inspired a group in Los Angeles to pray for an outpouring of the Holy Spirit for them and in April 1906 it says 'the fire fell' and the revival ran for around three years. This restored gifts of the Holy Spirit and there were miracles and healings with many caught up into a new dimension of the Spirit. In addition, believers began to speak in a heavenly language as they were baptised in the Holy Spirit and entered into a Spirit filled life. Not every church denomination was delighted with this development and it caused divisions resulting in yet more fragmentation of the church. But once again, there was no going back as God was moving the church forward again. Further moves of the Spirit have followed such as the Charismatic movement which saw the members of the traditional denominations, who had resisted Pentecostalism, begin to experience the works of the Holy Spirit themselves. Colin Urquhart who was an Anglican vicar in Luton experienced a revival bringing more understanding of the work of the Holy Spirit and what it means to be 'in Christ'. I believe we can expect more moves of the Holy Spirit as we approach the close of the age and our enemy looks to obstruct God's plans.

That is a brief skim over church history based on what different people have recorded for us, but what is the Bible perspective on church history from the end of the book of Acts? Let us consider the letters from Jesus to the seven churches contained in Revelation chapters 2 and 3. These address real problems that existed in those different places at that time but they are also meant to be read by all the other churches as each letter ends with: *'He who has an ear, let him hear what the Spirit says to the churches'*. There is also a personal application with the use of the singular word *'He who has an ear ...'*. In other words all the believers in that group of churches are to take note of what Jesus says. But does it have relevance for us today? There is an interpretation of these letters that gives them a prophetic dimension as the order and content of what Jesus said fits an understanding of church history. Let us see if there is any validity in this view and what it can tell us about the end of the church age. We will take each church in turn and in the order they are shown in the book of Revelation.

Ephesus

This is viewed as the church in the beginning when the apostles were still around. They had been diligent in their busyness for the Kingdom of Heaven but Jesus tells them that they had become too busy to remember Him. They were forgetting to love the One who first loved them. This was so serious that it seems they were in danger of no longer being considered a true church. This is a reminder to us that we always need to keep King Jesus central in our lives and the focus of our adoration. The mention of the Nicolaitans with their carnal attitudes may suggest their influence in the cooling of the church's love for Jesus.

Smyrna

The church in Smyrna pictures the time of increasing persecution of Christians. Successive Roman rulers through the first and second centuries sought to destroy the church. There is no rebuke from Jesus, He encourages them to keep going and remember the riches of the inheritance they have in Him. There is also the hint of the beginnings of the heresy that became Replacement Theology (i.e. Jews have been rejected by God and replaced by the Gentiles) with the words *'I know the slander of those who say they are Jews and are not, but are a synagogue of Satan.' (Revelation 2 v 9)*. There is still persecution of believers today which should encourage us to at least pray for them to be able to endure and also help them in whatever way we can.

Pergamum

Jesus commends believers here for holding fast to their faith in Him. But by referring to the Old Testament prophet Balaam, He exposes a problem that had come into the church. Balaam had advised an enemy king that the way to overthrow Israel was to entice them into idolatry and sexual immorality by mixing with the people of surrounding nations. Then God would lift His hand of protection because of their spiritual adultery and unfaithfulness to Him. The church in Pergamum was starting to mix ways of the world with their Christian lives. This is reminiscent of what happened when Constantine made Christianity the state religion which opened up the church to pagan practices. Jesus told us that the church is in the world but not of it, meaning that we are to be Spirit led, not led by fashion, culture, tradition or schemes of man. We need to guard against compromising with the world to try and blend in! The Nicolaitans are mentioned again which indicates that worldliness was a continuing problem in the church.

Thyatira

This was a church that Jesus commended for their continuing faith in Him and love which was demonstrated in their service for Him. But there was a serious problem which is illustrated by the reference to Jezebel who was wife of King Ahab of Israel. She was also the daughter of a pagan king promoting idolatry and sexual immorality amongst God's people. She was able to influence Ahab and exercised control over what went on in the land. She caused many problems through her manipulative behaviour. It seems that this same evil spirit had come into the church and Jesus is severe in His condemnation of the situation. If they do not drive out those who promote this behaviour and turn away from idolatry and immorality there will be great suffering. The emphasis appears to be that the church belongs to Jesus and He will act decisively to protect the honour of His name. There are echoes of the practices of the medieval church as popes exercised enormous political power and were able to manipulate kings throughout Europe. It was also a time of idolatry creeping into church practice illustrated by the worship of Mary as 'The Mother of God'. I think we still need an Elijah spirit (he confronted Jezebel) to see off any attempts to manipulate or control the church and to expose ungodly influences!

Sardis

This was a church that outwardly seemed to be healthy but the verdict of Jesus is that they are spiritually *'dead' (Revelation 3 v 1)*. He says that they need to wake up to their true condition, they need revival to restore true life to the church. They have done some things but He describes their deeds as incomplete. Jesus also says that if they don't respond He will *'come like a thief'* and at a time when they are not expecting Him. This could allude to the rapture, suggesting that this condition in the church may continue until believers are caught up to be with Him. There is also the comment that even in such churches there will be a remnant of true believers and that Jesus will not give up on them. I see this as fitting the church at the time of the Reformation. It may have restored the crucial truth of salvation by faith in Christ alone but it was incomplete in the sense that many other errors of doctrine were left unchanged. Furthermore it split the church into two camps, Catholic and Protestant and they were now violently opposed to each other destroying any unity in belief. In England it was simply a change of leadership. Henry VIII replaced the pope as head of the church to allow him to divorce and remarry as he wished but little else changed in practice. We can reasonably expect these two streams to endure until the rapture as they are so entrenched in world culture. We also remember that a remnant of true believers remained and despite the power struggles between the established religious leaderships they continued to fly the flag of truth. Men like John Knox of Scotland who insisted that salvation was more than a simple profession of faith and must be evidenced by changed lives. His influence produced a transformation in Scottish society.

Philadelphia

In this letter there are some rich truths to see. Jesus says *'I have placed before you an open door that no-one can shut' (Revelation 3 v 8)* which can be seen as the God arranged opportunities to preach the gospel to the world. Paul's missionary journeys are evidence of this. The comment that this church has *'little strength'* yet perseveres infers a reliance on the power of the Holy Spirit and not man's abilities. There is also the mention of *'those who claim to be Jews though they are not, but are liars'* seems to be a rebuke of Replacement Theology. Those who subscribe to this heresy would do well to remember that Jesus describes them as *'of the synagogue of Satan'* and He says they will be made to acknowledge their error. There is also the promise that this church will not enter the tribulation which is a clear indication that they will be raptured beforehand, a strong argument for the pre-tribulation interpretation of the end times. Again, when Jesus says *'I am coming soon'* it places this church at the end of the age. This is a missionary church and a return to its roots with its preaching of the gospel to the whole world. We can see in history how many different streams of the church established missionary movements to take the gospel out (e.g. Baptist Missionary Society). These denominational initiatives still exist today together with many other independent ministries throughout the world. That tells me that the Philadelphian church exists today and will do so until the rapture.

Laodicea

The dictionary defines someone who is laodicean as indifferent or half-hearted and that is exactly what Jesus says this church is like. He tells them that they are *'lukewarm' (Revelation 3 v 16)* which is a terrible indictment of their condition. It is so serious that He is about to spit them out of His mouth signalling His distaste for not only their deeds but their attitude. They even boast in their wealth and self-sufficiency. So what is the root cause of this condition? The name of the city means 'justice of the people' in Greek which reveals that man makes the decisions here not God. This has spilled over into the church, so much so that Jesus is not in the centre of their lives anymore as men rule the roost. There is no room for Him. This is revealed when He says *'Here I am! I stand at the door and knock. If anyone hears my voice and opens the door, I will come in and eat with him, and he with me.'* He is on the outside waiting to be invited in, but we also see God's grace shown to those caught up in this situation. If anyone hears and *'opens the door'* they will enjoy intimate communion with Him. This terrible state of this church most closely pictures the end time apostate church described by the apostle Paul in one of his letters: *'Let no one deceive you by any means; for that Day will not come unless the falling away comes first, and the man of sin is revealed, the son of perdition.'* *(2 Thessalonians 2 v 3 NKJV).* This explains that the rapture will not happen until there is the *'falling away'* which is what is known as the apostasy. The apostate church is a religious organisation but you will not find the Lord Jesus in it as everything is man centred. This type of church will exist at the end of the church age and will continue into the Tribulation.

This brings us to the end of our study of the letters to the seven churches in Revelation to see if the interpretation that they accurately describe church history is valid. I will leave you to decide if it is and whether it adds anything to our understanding of God's restoration plans for the church. There is one more subject that I will now cover.

This last restoration won't reach its fulfilment until the end of the Tribulation at the beginning of the millennium. This restoration is the bringing together of the church and Israel into one body. This will be a glorious moment when Jew and Gentile are united as one. Paul (a devout Jew and apostle to the Gentiles) explains this in his letter to the Ephesian church: *'For he* (Christ) *himself is our peace, who has made the two one and has destroyed the barrier, the dividing wall of hostility, by abolishing in his flesh the law with its commandments and regulations. His purpose was to create in himself one new man out of the two, thus making peace, and in this one body to reconcile both of them to God through the cross, by which he put to death their hostility'* *(Ephesians 2 v 14-16).* It has always been God's plan to bring Jew and Gentile believers together and everything necessary to make this possible has already been accomplished at the cross. The ancient hostility between the two has been dealt with. The Jews were defined by the Law of Moses and that separated them from all other nations, so Jesus did two things. First he fulfilled the Law for Israel, releasing them from all its religious requirements and second He opened up salvation to the Gentile world with the gospel. This truth challenges the continuing hostility to the Jews that exists in much of the church today. When we refuse to recognise this we are denying what God has planned. The church and Israel have been on two different paths but with a common destiny, unity. When the religious leaders of Israel rejected Jesus as their Messiah it opened up the age of the Gentile church. Israel were not forgotten by God but put to one side for a season. The Gentile church will be raptured before the Tribulation while Israel will go through it. When they are rescued from annihilation by the return of Jesus they will at last recognise Him as their Messiah then all Israel will be saved. At that point we will surely see the promised *'one new man'*. It must be said that there are Messianic Jews today and although few in number their numbers are growing and a prophetic picture of what is to come. We know that Jews have always been persecuted but these Jewish believers are experiencing even greater hostility particularly from Orthodox Jews. They need to experience acceptance by the church in recognition of what it says in Ephesians.

This brings me to the end of this look at God's redemption plans. Now it is time to think about what we do with this understanding. How should we be and what should we do?

CHAPTER 4: HOW SHOULD WE BE?

In the next two chapters we will look at what the Bible says about how we should be and what we should do in the light of the return of King Jesus. This has always been relevant for the church and even more so as world events are increasingly fulfilling end time prophecies. We are living in momentous times as the current world order is being shaken, sparking widespread anxiety about what will be the end of all this upheaval and uncertainty. As believers we have been given insight through the Bible into how things will unfold and how it will all end. This is not only for our own peace of mind but to shape our message for the world. I think we need to be like the men of Issachar who *'understood the times and knew what Israel should do.'* *(1 Chronicles 12 v 32)*. Understanding the times we live in is invaluable in preparing us for what is going to come.

I am drawing a distinction between how we should be and what we should do because they are two different things. What we do comes out of who we are which emphasises the importance of what we believe and think. Jesus put His finger on this when He said *'... out of the overflow of the heart the mouth speaks'* *(Matthew 12 v 34)*. In other words, what goes on inside us determines what we say and do. That is why I think it is important to study how we should be first before we look at what we do. What we know and think about God and His promises is crucial here, as pointed out by Paul *'Do not conform any longer to the pattern of this world, but be transformed by the renewing of your mind. Then you will be able to test and approve what God's will is – his good, pleasing and perfect will.'*

(Romans 12 v 2-3). All of us have a mindset that determines how we see things and shapes our attitude. These verses tell us to line up our thinking with what God says and not the world's ways, then we will be able to understand His perfect plans. We will now look at some different instructions in the Bible that relate to how we should be in the times we live in. But first I want to point out a foundational truth that will have a major impact on how we view what is happening today. This might not seem be the obvious place to start but I believe it is vital to protect us against being overwhelmed by fear and anxiety of end time events.

Be at peace

The first thing to know is that if we are believers we are at peace with God. Paul wrote *'... since we have been justified through faith, we have peace with God through our Lord Jesus Christ ...' (Romans 5 v 1)*. We should never undervalue the power of that truth. Faith in Christ gives us an inner peace that is unlike anything else and opens up our lives to God's favour and protection. Jesus said the peace He gives is not as the world gives but one rooted in His victory on the cross. As we read later *'... If God is for us, who can be against us? He who did not spare his own Son, but gave him up for us all – how will he not also, along with him, graciously give us all things? (Romans 8 v 31-32)*. To know, I mean really know that Almighty God is your perfect Father should cause fear and anxiety to evaporate. He is able and willing to take care of you in every situation and it is the revelation of His love for us that is the key to experiencing this peace. Again, Paul writes *'... God demonstrates his own love for us in this: While we were still sinners, Christ died for us.' (Romans 5 v 8)*. If we doubt that God loves we should see that He has demonstrated it in the most powerful way possible by surrendering His own beloved Son to the cross. We have peace with God because Jesus took responsibility for every sin we have ever committed or will commit. The barrier of sin has been removed by His once and for all sacrifice, for all sin, for all people to offer complete forgiveness of sin. And we receive a supernatural peace when we accept Jesus as our Saviour. This peace is enduring because as we believe in Him we are continually forgiven by the blood of Jesus that still speaks today (see Hebrews 12 v 24). Every time we take communion we are remembering that we are forgiven by the blood of Jesus in His onetime sacrifice for us. That is the foundation of peace we need in these perilous times and it is a precious gift that came through and in the person of the Lord Jesus Christ.

Be Wise

I can't think of a more important gift in perilous times than God's wisdom, which is the understanding of what to say or do. We know that when Solomon became king of Israel he asked God for wisdom to enable him to govern diligently. God not only granted his request by making him the wisest man of all time but gave him incredible favour in other things. The book of Proverbs (mostly written by Solomon) majors on the benefits of wisdom and includes this truth: *'Wisdom is supreme; therefore get wisdom. Whatever else you get, get understanding. Esteem her, and she will exalt you; embrace her, and she will honour you. She will set a garland of grace on your head and present you with a crown of splendour.' (Proverbs 4 v 7-9).* This makes wisdom a gateway gift to receiving God's grace for every possible situation, as Paul wrote: *'And God is able to make all grace abound to you, so that in all things at all times, having all that you need, you will abound in every good work.' (2 Corinthians 9 v 8).* Wisdom positions us to flow in that grace which will be so important in these days, not just for our own sakes but also for others we are able to help. But we are not left to our own devices as the Holy Spirit is the Spirit of wisdom. What in practice are we talking about?

When Jesus was talking to His disciples about signs of the end of the age, more than once He warned them about the danger of being deceived by false Christs and false prophets who would even be able to perform great signs and miracles (see Matthew 24 v 24). The context here is about the time of the Tribulation and the rise of the Antichrist. Jesus wants us to understand the signs of the times and put like this: *'Now learn this lesson from the fig tree: As soon as its twigs get tender and its leaves come out, you know that summer is near. Even so, when you see all these things, you know that it is near, right at*

CHAPTER 4: HOW SHOULD WE BE?

the door.' (Matthew 24 v 32-33). This also makes the point that it is events in Israel that give us the best understanding of where we are on God's clock. We are to pay attention to signs of the times so that we can discern what is really going on today. Discernment is a valuable gift of the Holy Spirit and is much needed in the church today, it will give us understanding that can feed into wisdom. As previously stated, one of Satan's strategies is to corrupt the church and he uses deceptive ideas to render it impotent or lead it into dangerous heresies, some of which we covered in the previous chapter. Also in the context of the end times Jesus encourages us to *'Therefore keep watch, because you do not know on what day your Lord will come.' (Matthew 24 v 42).* The parable of the Ten Virgins (Matthew 25) emphasises the need to 'stay awake' and be aware of what God is doing in the world today. I think this is best expressed as an Issachar ministry.

Desire

The apostle Peter in his letter about the end of the ages talks about looking forward to the culmination of all things. He wrote: *'But the day of the Lord will come like a thief. The heavens will disappear with a roar; the elements will be destroyed by fire, and the earth and everything in it will be laid bare. Since everything will be destroyed in this way, what kind of people ought you to be? You ought to live holy and godly lives as you wait eagerly for the day of God to come ...' (2 Peter 3 v 10-12).* He tells us to wait eagerly for all these overwhelmingly dramatic events to happen. As believers we know that it will be a time of rejoicing as we will have received our inheritance of eternal life with God in glory, but it will also be a terrifying time for those who reject Christ. That is why Peter is careful to preface this section by saying that God does not want anyone to perish but to turn to Him and accept Jesus as their Saviour. Given the enormity of all this can we truly say we wait eagerly for these things to come?

Studying this passage brought the seriousness of the current world situation into sharp focus for me. I am writing this as Russia is invading Ukraine and has already gained a foothold in Syria on the northern border of Israel. This prompts a big question: Is the present Russian regime the one that attacks Israel prior to the beginning of the millennium (as per the Ezekiel chapter 38 prophecy)? If it is, it suggests that the rapture and the Tribulation are on the near horizon and that this Russian regime will continue for at least another seven years (see earlier chapter on the end time doctrine I am working with). There are multiple indicators that the times are approaching the end with moves to global governance, a worldwide multi faith religion, increasing hostility to Israel and more. This is sobering stuff to consider and challenged me about my desire for the fulfilment of all this. Could I honestly say that I want all this to hurry up and happen? I was shocked that I could hesitate about this and realised that I was thinking the way the world does. This wasn't so much about what I wanted as I am in my seventies now but it was thinking about my family that had swayed me. My wife and I have grown up children and grandchildren and we naturally want them to live fulfilling lives and see their dreams realised but if the rapture happens now that will not happen for them. I realised that my mindset was wrong which had produced a hopelessly inadequate understanding of the wonder of being with the Lord Jesus in heaven. My mind needed renewing. The truth is, unfulfilled earthly desires are as nothing compared to the joy and true fulfilment of eternal life. Our children and grandchildren will not miss out on anything in heaven!

To sum up this section, I have concluded that the more revelation we have of the glory of the Lord Jesus and the wonder of heaven the more we will desire the fulfilment of the ages. We will also be impelled to preach the gospel with increasing urgency as we see the day approaching.

Be Ready

If we are to be ready for King Jesus we will need to be aware of the significance of the current world and church situation, subjects we covered in previous chapters. Just to remind ourselves: Jesus will come back twice, once to take the church to be with Him forever (the rapture)

CHAPTER 4: HOW SHOULD WE BE?

and then to deliver Israel from the jaws of destruction at the end of the Tribulation. These are two set events that are prophesied in the Bible which will affect every human being and determine their destiny. At the very least we need to know what the Bible promises about all this as burying our heads in the sand will not mean we escape their impact. Being aware is the prerequisite to being ready. What more can we learn about what that means?

The parable of the ten virgins waiting for the bridegroom recorded in Matthew 25 is an obvious example of being ready. Five wise ones took supplies of oil to replenish their lamps, so even though the bridegroom was a long time coming they were ready when he arrived. They were ready because they prepared themselves for however long was needed. It is easy to see a picture here of Jesus (as the bridegroom) coming for His bride (the church). In the gospel of Luke he groups together a collection of the teachings of Jesus. After a section on not worrying about the necessities of life he records a passage on being watchful. Jesus said: *'Be dressed ready for service and keep your lamps burning, like men waiting for their master to return from a wedding banquet, so that when he comes and knocks they can immediately open the door for him' (Luke 12 v 35-36)*. This is in a similar vein to the parable of the ten virgins by urging the servants to be ready by keeping watch as they wait. He later applies it specifically to His appearing: *'You also must be ready, because the Son of Man will come at an hour when you do not expect him.' (Luke 12 v 40)*. It is interesting that both these teachings are framed around a wedding which points to a wonderful event promised in the book of Revelation. It says: *'Let us rejoice and be glad and give him glory! For the wedding of the Lamb has come, and the bride has made herself ready.' (Revelation 19 v 7)*. This is the great celebration of the redeemed living in eternity with our Lord and Saviour Jesus Christ. I think back to when I was engaged when it was a time of making all the wedding arrangements, but what I remember most is the excitement and anticipation of living together with my wife for the rest of our lives. I was ready for the wedding! We can look forward with greater anticipation to our heavenly wedding celebration.

Let me conclude this chapter by making an observation about the early church who lived with the expectation of the return of Jesus. How did they maintain that hopeful mindset? See what they did: *'They devoted themselves to the apostles' teaching and to the fellowship, to the breaking of bread and to prayer.'* *(Acts 2 v 42)*. If we do what they did we too will be ready. And now we will look more at what we should do.

CHAPTER 5: WHAT SHOULD WE DO?

This chapter is not about what believers must do as that would be too legalistic. We will look at what we can do which is the theme of this book. I closed the last chapter by referring to what the church did at the very beginning after Pentecost. It says: *'They devoted themselves to the apostles' teaching and to the fellowship, to the breaking of bread and to prayer.' (Acts 2 v 42)*. To my mind that still stands as a good pattern for healthy church life. Furthermore, it says that they did these things every day and in their homes and the church grew rapidly as a result. This sounds radical to us with the pressures and demands of modern living but it does show how they geared their lives around their faith in Christ. Maybe it is not possible to structure our time in the same way but we can have the same mindset of living for Christ.

Those early believers put a premium on understanding what Christ had done and what that meant by being devoted to the apostles' teaching. It reminds us of the importance of sound preaching and teaching. We also have the added advantage of the New Testament which can give us personal revelation when the Holy Spirit opens up its meaning for us. They also met together continually which made it possible to support and encourage each other, particularly as they were being persecuted at the time. They had a community attitude which is at odds with our highly individualised modern culture. It poses the question as to whether we have lost something important that they had, the understanding that they were a body of people connected together through faith in Christ. Taking communion for them was something they did all the time, which would have helped them to keep focussed on the Saviour and what He had done on the cross. Communion today so often is relegated to an infrequent or scheduled religious ritual that loses the intimacy of the presence of Christ. Lastly it says they prayed and I can imagine that this was like a continuous conversation with God for them as well as times of communal prayer. After all didn't Jesus teach them: *'Ask and it will be given to you; seek and you will find; knock and the door will be opened to you. For everyone who asks receives; he who seeks finds; and to him who knocks, the door will be opened.' (Matthew 7 v 7-8).* They invited God into every situation as the book of Acts reveals.

The parable of the talents (Matthew 25) makes it clear that we are all given something to do in the Kingdom of Heaven. The simple interpretation here is that the master (Jesus) is going away for a time and instructs his servants (believers) to look after his business (preaching the gospel etc.) until he returns. They were not just to wait until he came back. We also note that there are different responsibilities given to the servants. This tells us that the callings God puts on our lives are tailor made for each of us as He calls us individually and equips us uniquely for what He wants us to do. We are not meant to be the same as each other and everyone's relationship with Jesus is different. Before we leave this parable there is the uncomfortable issue of the third uncooperative servant. He clearly didn't want to do what the master said and had a bad opinion of him. This disobedience meant he paid a heavy price for his wrong attitude. But this throws up an important point for us when we accept Jesus as our Saviour and Lord. At that moment we receive the forgiveness of sins together with the gift of eternal life and by making Him Lord we are also surrendering the whole of our lives to Him. Whether we realise it or not we have surrendered to Him all that we have so that He can lead us and work through us. But we are not taken over and made captive to His demands, we have entered an intimate relationship with a loving Saviour to live in harmony with Him. This flags up the question of where do our desires come in, are we to be resigned to reluctantly obeying His instructions. The answer is no as that is not what God wants. First of all, the plans He has for us are way better and more fulfilling than anything we could ever dream up. We can recall the promise where God says: '... "For I know the plans I have for you," declares the LORD, "plans to prosper you and not to harm you, plans to give you hope and a future..."' (Jeremiah 29 v 11). Although this was a promise to Israel in exile it is valid for all God's children. Secondly, when we surrender our lives to Him He starts a work in us that leads us to embrace what He wants to do in and through lives. See what Paul wrote: '... for it is God who works in you to will and to act according to his good purpose,' (Philippians 2 v 13). This means we desire to do what He says, not just because we love Him but it is what we want as well. That is when God provides the power to be successful in our calling. As a loving Father He only wants the best for us and it is another expression of His grace in our lives.

Another truth revealed in the verse from Philippians is that it is always God's power that matters and not man's abilities. Even any natural abilities we have are His doing as He is the Creator of life. Throughout the Old Testament we see God's Spirit empowering different people at certain times to carry out His will. After the cross the Holy Spirit came, first to live in us and then to work through us. As Jesus Himself said '... "Whoever believes in me, as the Scripture has said, streams of living water will flow from within him." By this he meant the Spirit, whom those who believed in him were later to receive. Up to that time the Spirit had not been given, since Jesus had not yet been glorified.' (John 7 v 38-39). At Pentecost the Holy Spirit came to empower us to do what Jesus asks and when we obey His power will always produce the right results. Paul that great preacher and teacher made it clear that any success he had was the work of the Holy Spirit as he wrote: 'My message and my preaching were not with wise and persuasive words, but with a demonstration of the Spirit's power, so that your faith might not rest on men's wisdom, but on God's power.' (1 Corinthians 2 v 4-5). This is timely advice for the modern church with all the impressive technology now available to support our activities. It has its place, but it is always God's power that makes the difference.

Now to a revelation that surprised me. In a passage on the end times the apostle Peter wrote: *'But the day of the Lord will come like a thief. The heavens will disappear with a roar; the elements will be destroyed by fire, and the earth and everything in it will be laid bare. Since everything will be destroyed in this way, what kind of people ought you to be? You ought to live holy and godly lives as you look forward to the day of God and speed its coming...' (2 Peter 3 v 10-12).* Notice the last phrase *'speed its coming'*, several other translations say 'hasten'. The dictionary defines the word hasten as meaning 'to cause to hurry'. The thought that we can affect the timing of these cataclysmic events is overwhelming. Can it be that God wants and gives us a responsibility to do things that hasten this day? I think there is a truth here but this is so big that we need some understanding to see if that is right. Paul makes an interesting comment about the birth of Jesus: *'But when the time had fully come, God sent his Son, born of a woman ...' (Galatians 4 v 4).* This prompts the question as to what had to happen to fulfil the timing. I have come to believe that God had to have prophets proclaim the coming of the Saviour to speak it into being just as God created by word in the beginning. At creation God delegated authority on earth to man and despite the disobedience in the Garden of Eden He stills works out His purposes through human beings. I always think of Simeon and Anna (a prophetess) earnestly praying and prophesying in the temple as they waited for the appearance of God's salvation for the world (see Luke 2). Were they the last link in the prophetic chain to fulfil the time? Another reason why our proclamations and prophesying are key is given by Paul: *'His* (God) *intent was that now, through the church, the manifold wisdom of God should be made known to the rulers and authorities in the heavenly realms, according to his eternal purpose which he accomplished in Christ Jesus our Lord.' (Ephesians 3 v 10-11).* This says that God works out His eternal purpose through the church and not independent from it. It means that our audience is not just people but spiritual powers and when we speak out God's words they have power to fulfil their purpose.

Let us think about these words: '... *so is my word that goes out from my mouth: It will not return to me empty, but will accomplish what I desire and achieve the purpose for which I sent it.*' *(Isaiah 55 v 11)*. Prophets spoke out God's words and they came to pass and the same is true today. If what I have argued is true then what can we do to hasten the day? Here are three obvious things.

Preach the gospel

This is the great commission given by Jesus and it remains our standing order. It was given to the first believers with the instruction to make Him known throughout the world and the book of Acts chronicles their efforts. When Jesus was talking to the disciples about the end of the age He put a dimension of timing on the preaching of the gospel: '*And this gospel of the kingdom will be preached in the whole world as a testimony to all nations, and then the end will come.*' *(Matthew 24 v 14)*. It is of course God who will determine the time of the end, but at the very least it means that our preaching of the gospel is a prerequisite for its fulfilment. Present day technology (television, internet, smart phones etc.) makes it possible to see this happen sooner.

A final thought on getting the good news of Jesus out is that the task of preaching the gospel isn't reserved for preachers alone. There are many ways the salvation message can be spread and through many different people and situations. Some people will never go into a church or attend a mission event but through day to day conversation they can open up to hear what you have to say, particularly when they are struggling with the challenges of life. And it can happen anywhere in the most unlikely places because that's where you find people! Like others, my wife has prayed for 'divine appointments' before she has gone out of the house and that has happened. One way or another the gospel will go out to all nations because Jesus said it would.

CHAPTER 5: WHAT SHOULD WE DO?

Proclamation

I pointed out earlier that I believe God wants and needs His as yet unfulfilled prophetic promises spoken into being. As the rapture and the other significant events leading up to the end of time are still to be fulfilled (as discussed in chapter 2) they need to be proclaimed. This is a very straightforward but powerful thing to do and can be done simply by reading the Bible out loud or in song. The important thing is that the prophecies are proclaimed whether in a church service or out in the world. To emphasise this I repeat the verse quoted earlier: *'... so is my word that goes out from my mouth: It will not return to me empty, but will accomplish what I desire and achieve the purpose for which I sent it.' (Isaiah 55 v 11)*. This might be a simple thing to do but God will use it to fulfil His plans.

Pray

This is a very obvious point but needs to be made. The simplest heartfelt prayer we can make is the one that closes the book of Revelation: *'Come, Lord Jesus.' (Revelation 22 v 20)*. It expresses our desire for the times to be fulfilled so we can be face to face with our Lord Jesus forever. But we know that there are momentous events yet to take place in the world that we have looked at in this book and we can't pray that they won't happen. However there is something to see about how they happen. Jesus told His disciples about the extreme persecution that would come in the Tribulation triggered by the Antichrist raising himself up to be god in the temple in Jerusalem. When this takes place He tells people to quickly escape to the mountains (probably referring to Edom which is present day Jordan). He comments that this will be dreadful for pregnant women and nursing mothers as it is obviously going to be extremely difficult for them in this situation. But while these terrible things will definitely happen Jesus says: *'Pray that your flight will not take place in the winter or on the Sabbath.' (Matthew 24 v 20)*. So while we cannot ask God to stop them happening we are told to pray how things will unfold. If they have to flee in winter it will be harder because some could perish in the cold weather. If they flee on a Sabbath it will be obvious to everyone as they break the rules limiting the distance they can travel on that day, and if noticed they could be caught before they reach safety. This should inform all our praying in the end times so that no-one unnecessarily suffers or even needlessly perish.

Let me close this chapter with a radical thought. If we really believe that in the rapture all true believers alive at that time will suddenly disappear from sight leaving behind an apostate church of nominal Christians and a surprised world, shouldn't we make sure they understand what has happened. Satan will work overtime to spread false ideas about where we have gone (e.g. abducted by aliens) as he is terrified of the implications, because he knows his time of freedom is short. We could post a message pointing people to the Bible explanation of the rapture and the importance of believing in the Saviour. We could leave it with the instruction 'to be opened in the event of our disappearance'! It will not be too late for those who remain to put their trust in Jesus and receive their salvation. They have been referred to as Tribulation Saints. This is consistent with God's heart as he is *'not wanting anyone to perish, but everyone to come to repentance.'* (2 Peter 3 v 9). This leads us into our next chapter when we consider what is our message to the world in these end days?

CHAPTER 6: WHAT IS OUR MESSAGE?

In the light of all that will happen in the end times, what is our message to the world? We are living in times when terrible things are happening and there is increasing ungodliness throughout the world. There are even laws being implemented that are not only blatantly against what the Bible says but seem to make no sense to reasonable thinking. This isn't restricted to oppressive regimes with extreme ideologies but is happening in democracies where people have a say over who governs them. The driving force behind all this is Satan, as Paul wrote: *'The god of this age has blinded the minds of unbelievers, so that they cannot see the light of the gospel of the glory of Christ, who is the image of God.'* *(2 Corinthians 4 v 4)*. We are in a spiritual battle and simply trying to persuade people and authorities to act righteously will not turn things around. People will only live differently when they are born again through faith in Christ. While it is true that the church has much to say about all the controversial issues that the modern world is obsessed with, we often see that our stand for the truth is ignored and even used to vilify us. There is nothing new in this, particularly when we talk about Jesus coming again, see what Peter wrote: *'First of all, you must understand that in the last days scoffers will come, scoffing and following their own evil desires. They will say "Where is this 'coming' he promised? Ever since our fathers died, everything goes on as it has since the beginning of creation."' (2 Peter 3 v 3-4)*. So what should our response be to all the ungodliness we see? Don't misunderstand me, it is good that we speak up against injustice and unrighteousness but it is not the prime message that Jesus gave us to

CHAPTER 6: WHAT IS OUR MESSAGE?

take to the world. In the simplest terms it is to make Jesus known and we do that with the gospel. We are not called to straighten the world out but to be lights in the darkness. Our enemy always wants to distract us from preaching the message of salvation and get us entangled in all manner of contentious debates that won't change people's destinies.

This brings us to a big point, and it is that the gospel is an eternal message. Every human being has an eternal destiny either with God or cut off from God, and there is no such thing as oblivion or nothing. To be blunt, there is a heaven and there is a hell but God wants everyone with Him in heaven which is why He sent His Son into the world. If we are honest, even the church can be reluctant to speak about death and eternal destinies and it will be helpful to consider why that is. One obvious reason is the fear of death which makes people shy away from thinking about it and the lack of understanding only reinforces their anxiety. But we, the church, have a message that can liberate them, see this promise: *'Since the children have flesh and blood, he* (Jesus) *too shared in their humanity so that by his death he might destroy him who holds the power of death – that is, the devil – and free those who all their lives were held in slavery by their fear of death.' (Hebrews 2 v 14-15).* The Lord Jesus became a man and experienced human death to break the power of it for us, so that we no longer need to fear it. At the end of a true believer's life on earth their spirit leaves their body to be with Jesus forever. Look at this amazing statement by Jesus: *'I tell you the truth, if anyone keeps my word, he will never see death.' (John 8 v 51).* Death here is portrayed as a spirit that believers won't even see. In the book of Revelation death and hades (hell) are personified as evil spirits that are destined for destruction (see Revelation 6 v 8 and 20 v 14). This is part of our gospel message. But I think there is another reason why eternal destiny is not talked about more. We have all heard amazing testimonies of people whose lives have been radically changed when they believed in Jesus as their Saviour. People have been freed from addictions, incurable illnesses, suicidal thoughts, lives of violence and every other distressing human experience. When these stories are told they have a powerful effect in evangelism and will have played a part in the salvation of many who experience a new life in the world. But salvation isn't just for this life but also for the life to come. Paul made a comment about this: *'If only for this life we have hope in Christ, we are to be pitied more than all men.' (1 Corinthians 15 v 19).* Here he was countering the lie that there is no resurrection of the dead, which would mean that death is the end of all things even for believers. This is not true as there is a promised resurrection to eternal life. We need to make sure we don't forget this truth of eternity by being preoccupied with life now, even when we are overwhelmed by problems.

So what is our message to the world? Even though the modern era is so different to the time the gospel first went out, the message has not changed. Here are the words of Jesus:

"For God so loved the world that he gave his one and only Son, that whoever believes in him shall not perish but have eternal life. For God did not send his Son into the world to condemn the world, but to save the world through him. Whoever believes in him is not condemned, but whoever does not believe stands condemned already because he has not believed in the name of God's one and only Son."' (John 3 v 16-18).

This continues to be our simple message to the world. The gospel gives people the opportunity to move from death to life by accepting Jesus as their Saviour. The result is: *'Yet to all who received him, to those who believed in his name, he gave the right to become children of God – children born not of natural descent, nor of human decision or a husband's will, but born of God' (John 1 v 12-13).* I will let those words speak for themselves.

While the message hasn't changed and doesn't need to, there is something to say about what is happening in the world right now. Wars, pandemics and economic instability has created an epidemic of anxiety and sense of hopelessness. The gospel is the biggest message of hope there has ever been. Peter wrote these words: *'Praise be to the God and*

CHAPTER 6: WHAT IS OUR MESSAGE?

Father of our Lord Jesus Christ! In his great mercy he has given us new birth into a living hope through the resurrection of Jesus Christ from the dead, and into an inheritance that can never perish, spoil or fade – kept in heaven for you, who through faith are shielded by God's power until the coming of the salvation that is ready to be revealed in the last time.' (1 Peter 1 v 3-5). The gospel is the message of hope we hold out to the world. Amen.

CHAPTER 7:
FINAL THOUGHTS

At the last supper Jesus told His disciples to share bread and wine together as the way of remembering Him and we recognise this as the act of communion celebrated in church today. But it is worth pointing out that for the early church it was done as they met together in their own homes (see Acts 2 v 46) emphasising their desire to keep their focus on the Saviour and what He had done for them at the cross. When Jesus was teaching about the coming of the Holy Spirit He said: *'He* (the Holy Spirit) *will bring glory to me by taking from what is mine and making it known to you.' (John 16 v 14).* This tells us that the Holy Spirit will always point us to Jesus as He wants Him to be the focus of our worship and the consistent theme of our preaching. We have many things we can justifiably teach on in church but they should all be done in a way that glorifies Jesus. These words from the book of Hebrews encourage us to make Him centre stage in our lives: *'Let us fix our eyes on Jesus, the author and perfecter of our faith, who for the joy set before him endured the cross, scorning its shame, and sat down at the right hand of the throne of God.' (Hebrews 12 v 2).* This is trustworthy advice in our perilous times.

The Lord Jesus will come again twice more. The first time to take the true church to be with Him and the second time to deliver His people Israel from destruction. Before Jesus came the first time John the Baptist was sent ahead of Him to prepare the way and he was the fulfilment of this prophecy from Isaiah: *'A voice of one calling: "In the desert prepare the way for the LORD; make straight in the wilderness a highway for our*

CHAPTER 7: FINAL THOUGHTS

God. Every valley shall be raised up, every mountain and hill made low; the rough ground shall become level, the rugged places a plain. And the glory of the LORD will be revealed, and all mankind together will see it. For the mouth of the LORD has spoken.'" (Isaiah 40 v 3-5). This has an end time dimension to it and it will not be completely fulfilled until Jesus comes the last time. John the Baptist had the task at His first coming and now I see us having that same call before the rapture. In the book of Revelation it indicates that Jewish witnesses will do the same before His third coming (see Revelation 11). I am convinced that more than ever the church has been given a preparation ministry.

As we wait for the promised return of the KING OF KINGS AND LORD OF LORDS we would do well to take note of Paul's letter to Titus which says: *'For the grace of God that brings salvation has appeared to all men. It teaches us to say "No" to ungodliness and worldly passions, and to live self-controlled, upright and godly lives in this present age, while we wait for the blessed hope – the glorious appearing of our great God and Saviour, Jesus Christ, who gave himself for us to redeem us from all wickedness and to purify for himself a people that are his very own, eager to do what is good.' (Titus 2 v 11-14).* The defining issue here is the revelation of the grace of God given to us in Jesus Christ and the more we enter into this grace the more we will see His power at work in us as we prepare for the coming of the King.

I will end with this: *'Now to him who is able to do immeasurably more than all we ask or imagine, according to his power that it is at work within us, to him be glory in the church and in Christ Jesus throughout all generations, for ever and ever! Amen.' (Ephesians 3 v 20-21).*

ABOUT THE AUTHOR

Christopher Bomford lives in North Yorkshire with his wife Heather. They have been married for over 50 years and have two grown up daughters and four grandchildren. They have both been involved in church leadership in Essex as pastors, inter-church initiatives and children's work.

Since moving to West Yorkshire in 2006 they have been involved with several different fellowships as they continue to hold to their desire to work with all denominations. Christopher has continued preaching and teaching what the Bible says to us today. A recent move to North Yorkshire has led them to The Hollybush Christian Fellowship near Thirsk, where they are currently based.

This joins his first book **Berean Letters** which was published in 2022.